BECOME
INSPIRED

BECOME
INSPIRED

JAY STYLES

BLACK WALL STREET
PUBLISHING

Library of Congress Control Number: 2021900854

Styles, Jay, author. Become Inspired: Your Next Steps, A simple but powerful guide to shifting your mindset, sparking inspiration and reaching your goals in only 11 weeks / Jay Styles

Publisher's Cataloging-In-Publication Data

(Prepared by The Donohue Group, Inc.)

Names: Styles, Jay, author.

Title: Become inspired : your next steps : a simple but powerful guide to shifting your mindset, sparking inspiration and reaching your goals in only 11 weeks / Jay Styles.

Description: Los Angeles, California : Black Wall Street Publishing, [2021]

Identifiers: ISBN 9781736493601 (trade paperback) | ISBN 9781736493618 (trade hardback) | ISBN 9781736493625 (ebook) | ISBN 9781736493632 (Kindle)

Subjects: LCSH: Inspiration. | Positive psychology. | Goal (Psychology) | Visualization. | Success--Psychological aspects.

Classification: LCC BF410 .S79 2021 (print) | LCC BF410 (ebook) | DDC 153.3--dc23

City of Publication: Los Angeles, California

Black Wall Street Publishing books are available at special discounts for bulk purchases in the US by corporations, institutions and other organizations For more information, contact Black Wall Street Publishing at books@blackwallstreetpublishing.com

Acknowledgments

I want to acknowledge my wife, Monica, who has believed in me since day one; my parents, Phyllis and Larry Raines; my dad, Cecil Fowler; my siblings, Corey Batey, Eboni Fowler, Jada Raines; my new friend Barak, for helping me with the outline for this book; and all of my immediate family and friends, who have supported me by attending an event I hosted, listening to me ramble on the airwaves, watching and sharing my red-carpet interviews on social media, giving me a word or two of encouragement, sending me direct messages on social media expressing pride in me, and always supporting my new endeavors no matter what they were. It is because of your support that I am able to continue to get up and dust myself off after falling down again and again. So, from the bottom of my heart, thank you!

CONTENTS

INTRODUCTION

Feeling lost and need some inspiration to keep pushing toward your goal? Do you find yourself stuck in your career and you just can't seem to move to the next level? Are you comparing your success to the success of your peers? Are you ready to move forward with your passion project, but procrastination has set in over not knowing where to start? Have you ever been inspired by someone who has faced worse circumstances in life than you, yet they somehow find ways to overcome those circumstances and still pursue their passions and live out their dreams? What about when you watch those short, uplifting pieces on network TV of people who are facing a terminal illness or a life-changing amputation and are still determined to pursue the things that make them happy, taking back control of their life and living it on their terms? Do they inspire you to take that first step toward your dream? If not, what's stopping you?

ESPN features their E60: inspirational stories weekly and a couple of years back they featured two wrestlers and high

1

school teammates from Cleveland: Dartanyon Crockett, who is legally blind—born with Leber's disease, an inherited eye condition—and Leroy Sutton, whose legs were amputated at the age of eleven after being pulled beneath a train traveling at 49 miles per hour. The two were much more than teammates as Dartanyon would carry Leroy around on his back through school hallways and during wrestling matches. What most inspired me was Dartanyon and Leroy's mindset. They identified that they were being challenged and decided not to let that break them. They chose to live life on their terms by facing their challenges head-on.

This is what separates those who are living inspiring lives from those who are inspired from afar by watching others overcome their circumstances. The willpower to choose between taking your life back versus being bogged down in self-pity, fear, uncertainty, frustration, procrastination, or whatever feelings strike you at that moment to prevent you from redirecting that same energy into taking small steps toward your dreams, shrinking those negative emotions until they're no longer there.

Before I started the docuseries *Become Inspired*, I was bogged down by many uncertainties about the series: How many episodes should I have? What should I title the show? What is the tone and look of the show? Should I be on camera in the series or just the guest? Where will I get the finances to fund the series? What type of guest should I have on the show? I realized I needed to take a step back, breathe, and focus on one thing at a time. By taking baby steps, I figured out the first uncertainty, then I moved on to the next one. The further I got down the list, the less overwhelmed I was by that feeling of uncertainty, until it no longer existed and I was no longer bogged down. Instead, those negative feelings of uncertainty evolved into a big ball of excitement that fueled my confidence until nothing seemed too big, which then also fueled my creative juices so much that great ideas for the series came from every direction. It appeared as if they were falling from the sky.

This inspirational guide is nothing more than a blueprint to shifting your mindset and staying inspired to really live life on your terms despite the curveballs life throws your way. This book includes different setbacks and challenges I faced in my life as well as examples from each guest in my Amazon Prime *Become Inspired* series and using them as a guide and lesson plan to overcome those same challenges in your life. At the end of each chapter, there will be specific exercises to highlight how these concepts can be applied to your life to overcome those different emotions you're probably feeling.

Instead of reading this guide all in one sitting, I recommend spending one week on each chapter and completing the exercises. Take that week to meditate on what you've read, apply the exercises to your circumstances, and then move to the next week.

During the implementation of strategies discussed in chapters one through eleven, you'll discover and maximize your inner greatness to do and accomplish things that once defeated you.

To keep you accountable, you'll find a contract that is a promise to yourself to follow through with the weekly exercises even when you're faced with a tough week. Be sure to sign and date the contract, then come back to it when you need the encouragement to go on.

BECOME INSPIRED: YOUR NEXT STEPS CONTRACT

I, _____, understand that this inspirational guide is a step toward accomplishing my goals and realizing my dreams by changing my mindset as well as my behavior. However, only reading the guide without completing the weekly exercises at the end of each chapter not only gives the guide an injustice, but I am cheating myself out of maximizing my inner greatness.

I, _____, understand that by taking my time and reading a chapter a week, while also completing the exercises, I benefit more than by trying to read the entire guide all in one sitting.

I, _____, commit to the weekly readings as well as the completion of the weekly exercises to the best of my abilities no matter how I'm feeling or the type of week I'm having.

I, _____, understand that mastering these exercises will take time, but I'm committed and will trust the process.

I, _____, am committed to changing my mindset, self-talk, and bad habits weekly as I complete the guide in its entirety.

_____

(Signature)

_____

(Date)

GOOD HABITS, BAD HABITS

You must first forget Inspiration.
Creating the habit is more dependable.
Habits will sustain you whether you're inspired or not.

CHRISTINA BRYANT @THEPRETTYLIFTA

As I was scrolling on Instagram, I came across a post from an old friend in college who is now a bodybuilder. She published a photo of herself in her bodybuilder stance, showing off her toned and defined physique with the caption: "You must first forget inspiration. Creating the habit is more dependable. Habits will sustain you whether you're inspired or not."

That caption blew my mind, and I felt it was only right to share it with you because of its truth. Inspiration eventually wears off, but the repetition of good habits stays with you for the long haul. Christina's starting weight was 230 pounds, while her current weight at the time was 130 pounds. She needed more than just inspiration to transform her physique into the person she is today; she needed the daily repetition of good habits to become disciplined.

We all have them whether they're good or bad; habits will either reward us with an outcome of success and prosperity or do the exact opposite and impede our progress. Believe it or not, it is possible to be inspired and practice bad habits; inspiration alone is not enough to take action. Taking action requires a level of discipline from practicing good habits so that when you are inspired, you have the discipline to follow through to the end goal.

Ten years ago, when I was working as a radio personality in Columbus, Georgia, I had great career aspirations, such as writing a book on my struggles as a college student that led to where I was in my career at that time. But I lacked the discipline to plan out my writing schedule or even to create an outline for my book. I was too lazy to write my own book; instead, I hired a ghostwriter, and we would weekly record my responses to the questions she asked me and would later transcribe for the book.

In short, the book was never finished because I lacked the discipline to follow through on the weekly meetups, on top of the many bad habits I practiced, all of which halted my progress. This may sound silly, but at that time I believed success was supposed to happen to me somewhat magically because of the household name I had built for myself around town. I had my head in the clouds. In my mind, my book was supposed to happen because I said it was going to happen, but not by actually putting in the work and developing good habits to make it happen. I wasted five hundred bucks on the idea of how cool it would be to become an author and adding another accolade to my list of accomplishments. That was definitely the wrong type of thinking, not to mention a waste of time for the person I hired to write the book, who could have been working with someone more serious. Comedian Kevin Hart has a saying: "Everyone wants to be successful, but don't nobody wants to put in the work."

It's mind-boggling to think that bad habits are easier to develop than good habits, even when you realize that they're what's keeping you stuck in the same place or, worse, jeopardizing your health. But we see it happen every day in our own lives as well as observing others around us. I'm definitely not a behavioral psychologist, but from developing bad habits of my own over the years, I can tell you there are only two reasons for it: stress and procrastination.

When we're stressed, we often resort to bad habits to suppress our feelings and take our minds off the stressor. In actuality, we're just feeding the ugly monster of bad habits until it becomes so enormous it's almost impossible to stop. That is, until it's replaced by a good habit, which we'll discuss toward the conclusion of this chapter. We are all different in how we suppress our emotions; some of us suppress by smoking, some by drinking, some by sex, some by drugs, and others by food.

Procrastination is often the precursor to fearing the unknown. By not following through in a timely and well-organized manner, we avoid any criticism or failure we might encounter, yet this form of inaction or "later" thinking always comes with a price. We've all practiced procrastination in a variety of ways, whether it's deciding to binge-watch your favorite show instead of getting started on your business plan, telling yourself that you'll start your day going to the gym but staying in bed until it's time to go to work, choosing to scroll on social media instead of working on your goals for the new year, or choosing happy hour over putting time into your goals. How many times have you been motivated to start your own business, but fear sets in, so everything that you had in motion gets put on the back burner because fear of failure or fear of ridicule took over?

Earlier in my career, procrastinating was hard for me to admit to, but when I finally recognized that I had a problem with it, my life began to change, and I was able to start following through on my goals. For me, in order to find out why I was procrastinating, I simply had to be honest with myself and realize that the dreams I set out for myself were so big, I had no clue on how I would ever accomplish something of that magnitude and had no idea where I would even start.

I was procrastinating out of fear and uncertainty, and I knew if I didn't shake myself out of this terrible habit, my dreams would never see the light of day. Plus, I would be a miserable old man telling "should've" and "could've" stories to my future grandkids or anyone that could bear to listen.

TAKING BABY STEPS

In order for me to get out of my procrastination slump, I needed to develop the mindset that small steps are just as important as big steps. By dedicating small steps toward my goals every day, I would be that much closer to accomplishing my goal. It's really just that simple. I found that this simple change in mindset allowed me to overcome the fear of the unknown and learn to be diligent and just start, even when I didn't have the slightest idea what I was doing.

When I decided that I was going to write this book, I had no clue where to start, or how I was going to format the book, or better yet, how I'd get the book published. I asked myself all of these questions as the fear of the unknown started to bubble up inside. Recognizing my old patterns, I quickly changed my mindset to figuring it out step-by-step and day by day. That new process allowed me to take the baby steps of researching book outlines that authors use to organize all of their ideas on paper, making it easier for them to start writing. Taking another small step, I'd figure out how to publish my book as well as the pre publishing process. Believe it or not, achieving these small goals really boosted my confidence, and I was no longer in the dark about how to get this book done, instead, I was anxious to complete it because I finally had the courage and drive necessary to push me through. Taking baby steps and using the resources available to me were key to starting my passion project.

UTILIZING YOUR RESOURCES

There was a time I depended upon a mentor or someone who had already walked the path that I wanted to walk. Then one day I realized that Google was my best friend—as well as a billion other people's—and a great resource. Just think about it, whatever you want to learn is really only a Google search away.

The internet is so readily accessible that we forget to maximize this resource before looking for others to help us. There are sites, such as Udemy and Skillshare, specifically designed to teach a skill or a particular subject. Not to mention free services like YouTube where you can find just about anything, including numerous how-to videos.

In season one, episode one, of *Become Inspired*, entrepreneur and director Christina Cooper says this: "If people are not going to help you, you have to do it on your own." In some cases, you may have a mentor or friend you can go to in the beginning for guidance and that's a plus, but often you have to navigate the waters on your own and maximize every internet search, tutorial, or book you can get your hands on to guide you on your journey.

WEEK ONE EXERCISES

This first week I want you to become familiar with your "good habits" as well as your "bad habits," then write them down using the section on the next page. I really want you to be honest with yourself and list as many bad habits as you can first, then go and write down some of your good habits.

If you have more bad habits than good habits, no need to feel bad about it, this is the first step toward change. I then want you to evaluate your bad habits and identify the *cue, routine,* and the *reward*, which is explained through an example below.

I came across an article written by coach and human behavior professor Melody Wilding, and she had this to say about changing bad habits: "If you don't first understand the psychology driving habits, you'll never see any real success." That makes perfect sense. If you don't understand what drives the habit, then you won't know how to shake off the habit.

Exercise One

Identify all three stages of your bad habits. For example, you've worked a long, exhausting week (cue), which prompts you to relax for the weekend (routine) and get through two seasons of *Game of Thrones* (reward).

Exercise Two

Write down healthier alternative behaviors that will produce the results you want. For example, what alternative behavior might provide a comparable reward to the one you're trying to eliminate? Maybe binge-watching your favorite series gives you a sense of relaxation and happiness, but so does working diligently on your passion project and the sense of accomplishment that it brings. So write that down and replace the TV binge-watching.

Exercise Three

Write down any setbacks that may affect the process, then make adjustments in your schedule as needed. For instance, if you have to go into work this weekend or you're scheduled to work, block off some time to focus on your passion project, and pick up speed again when your schedule reverts back to normal.

USE THE NEXT COUPLE OF PAGES TO COMPLETE THE EXERCISE

Write down five of your good habits as well as your bad habits.

GOOD HABITS	BAD HABITS
1.	1.
2.	2.
3.	3.
4.	4.
5.	5.

EXERCISE ONE

Identify all three stages of your bad habits using the *cue, routine*, and *reward* method.

Cue: anything that triggers a behavior
(time, location, people, events)

Routine: any behavior triggered by the cue

Reward: a sense of accomplishment

BAD HABIT 1:		
CUE (triggers: time, location, people, events):	**ROUTINE:**	**REWARD:**

BAD HABIT 2:		
CUE (triggers: time, location, people, events):	**ROUTINE:**	**REWARD:**

BAD HABIT 3:		
CUE (triggers: time, location, people, events):	ROUTINE:	REWARD:

BAD HABIT 4:		
CUE (triggers: time, location, people, events):	ROUTINE:	REWARD:

BAD HABIT 5:		
CUE (triggers: time, location, people, events):	ROUTINE:	REWARD:

EXERCISE TWO

Write down some healthier (routine) alternative behaviors using the responses from the last exercise.

UNHEALTHY BEHAVIOR (ROUTINE) 1:	HEALTHY BEHAVIOR ALTERNATIVE:

UNHEALTHY BEHAVIOR (ROUTINE) 2:	HEALTHY BEHAVIOR ALTERNATIVE:

UNHEALTHY BEHAVIOR (ROUTINE) 3:	HEALTHY BEHAVIOR ALTERNATIVE:

UNHEALTHY BEHAVIOR (ROUTINE) 4:	HEALTHY BEHAVIOR ALTERNATIVE:

UNHEALTHY BEHAVIOR (ROUTINE) 5:	HEALTHY BEHAVIOR ALTERNATIVE:

EXERCISE THREE

Write down your schedule for this week and include any possible conflicts that may affect your productivity.

_____

_____

_____

_____

_____

_____

_____

_____

_____

_____

_____

_____

_____

_____

2

ALL THINGS WORK TOGETHER FOR THE GOOD

Whatever is working against your dreams, is actually working for you. You just don't know it yet.

UNKNOWN

There was a time when I was numb to the phrase, "All things work together for the good." Not because I heard it every Sunday morning from the preacher in the pulpit, and definitely not because it was a phrase used by everyone so loosely in the moment of comfort, but because I didn't want to understand how something that went completely against my dreams and desires would actually work in my favor one day. How could that possibly be true?

It wasn't until I was forced out of a career that was sucking the life out of me, that had dealt me disappointment after disappointment with years of hard work and nothing to show for it, that I realized sometimes steps that seem to take you backwards are actually taking you on a different path toward your dream. Upon relocating to Los Angeles, I was still in a lower level position at the radio station, and no matter how well I performed, I was always overlooked when a higher position became open. I was mentally defeated and spiritually broken, but this mental episode allowed me to spend more time meditating and talking with God about my true purpose, which helped lead me out of the dark place I was in. A few months after I was laid off from the radio station, the universe started to send me signs that my next adventure was creating television shows that were inspiring and uplifting. I realized that my experience in entertainment prepared me for my new adventure, and I just needed to trust the process. I was equipped with all the skills necessary to make this new adventure a reality.

My experience in entertainment honed both my writing and communication skills, but it also allowed me to pick up new skills, such as the basics of video editing as well as understanding camera functions and how to film my own content if needed.

The one thing that was essential to my success as a writer and a producer was doing due diligence and researching the ins and out of television and distinguishing what makes great television by understanding the elements involved. I was already equipped with the rest of the skills to get started. And that's what I did.

Before I moved to Los Angeles, I had a vision of creating television and started the process of researching using the TV Writers Vault website, which gave me a step-by-step process on creating both scripted and unscripted television. God even sent me the vision in a dream one night, making my purpose crystal clear, but somehow I convinced myself that being a radio personality was the path for me, so I ignored the dream.

As I think about it now, I feared the possibilities of where this dream could have taken me. Instead, I opted for the familiar path because it brought me a level of comfort.

It's fair to say that whatever it is you're supposed to be doing—your true purpose—the universe will circle back around and find you again in mysterious ways, whether through a dream, coincidence, or through signs guiding you closer toward your purpose. Just know that when you do move closer to your true purpose, you may not realize it at the time, but you've been preparing for this unwittingly for months, or maybe years. We tend to think we've lost so much time chasing the inevitable that it's impossible to catch up with our own true purpose.

But in reality, you are where you are supposed to be, and although your path was detoured, it has prepared your skills and your mindset to better serve your true purpose.

Jason Carter, former entertainment host who worked for Entertainment Tonight online, talked about this in episode four of season one of *Become Inspired*, and how he was on the verge of giving up and going back to school when he received a phone call that changed his life. I've heard testaments like these before and, believe it or not, the blessing always comes right before your breaking point, proving that God or the universe, whichever you believe in, is always on time.

POSITIONING YOURSELF

It's one thing to say you have a desire to accomplish your goals, but it's another thing when you are willing to position yourself for opportunities that can take you places. Before moving to Los Angeles, I knew I wanted more from my career. I wanted to move mountains and accomplish things that I never thought I could possibly do, and I knew that meant putting myself in places for things to happen, even if it would make me uncomfortable.

And just to clarify, positioning yourself does not mean moving across the globe, but rather aligning your steps with that of the goals you want to accomplish so that opportunities can present themselves. Putting yourself in places for things to happen is an essential recipe for success; it gives you a sense of peace that something is bound to happen because you're on the right path. If your goal is to be a TV host, how have you positioned yourself to accomplish this goal? Have you invested in classes? Have you invested in a camera and microphone so you can film your own 'man on the street' interviews? What about if you're looking to switch careers, how have you positioned yourself? Have you taken classes to get certified? Have you gone back to school? What about if you want to start a business? How have you positioned yourself to set up a business plan?

How much time are you putting in working on your business after your nine-to-five job? Have you come up with an exit strategy when you transition from your "job" to your dream career?

These are the questions I ask myself every day to keep me on track toward a goal. Being honest with yourself and making the necessary changes will get you that much closer. We all have control over the life we can envision for ourselves, and we have the ability to manifest the dreams we desire. In order to change our reality, though, we have to position ourselves for those dreams to happen.

STAY THE COURSE

It can be difficult to stay on course without detouring to other things, especially when you hit roadblocks and obstacles in your path. But staying the course is a prerequisite for great things to come. Staying the course can be difficult when you're doing the work but not seeing any doors open for you. However, it's important to learn and celebrate the small victories to stay encouraged and inspired in continuing the journey.

Small victories can be anywhere, from finding a logo designer for your business, enrolling back in school, getting certified, getting accepted into that program, or even breaking a bad habit or two. These are all victories you should take great pride in and will give you the confidence to take the next step toward success.

As an entrepreneur, I've been looking for new ways to bring in more streams of income. And just last week I had an idea for a new app, which I can't go into just yet, but will allow me to receive passive income. The idea hit me as I was looking to solve a problem and did some research and found that no other app out there is offering this type of service. I had no knowledge of how to build an app or where to even start. So, I needed to either find someone who has experience building apps or find a book that goes into detail on how to start an app business. I found a great book on app entrepreneurship and read it within a week. After reading the book, my confidence grew because now I understood the structure of this new business and the next baby step to take.

Sometimes the small victories can come from educating yourself on what it is you need to do next. As your confidence begins to build, you become more motivated to move forward until you've accomplished your goal.

WEEK TWO EXERCISES

Take this week to go back and really think about the accomplishments in your personal and professional life—no matter how small you think they are. Reflect, reflect, and reflect some more.

Exercise One

Get a sheet of paper and tear it into strips (big enough that you can write on). Next, find an empty Mason jar (you can get these at the grocery store or order online). Write down all your small victories for either this week or the previous week and place them in the jar. Store the jar somewhere visible so you can see it every day. Add your small victories to your victory jar daily, and when you're faced with a bad day or negative thought, grab the jar and take out one of those strips of paper and read it.

Exercise Two

In this chapter, I suggested putting yourself in a position to win, so think about the goals you want to accomplish. It could be starting a business, writing a book, losing weight—whatever goal you want to set for yourself. Remember that you have to start somewhere, so think about how you could get started on these goals, and write down some of the steps it will take to reach your goal. You may have to research, but that's an action step in itself, and one that's placing you in a position to win. Focus on three action steps you can take to get closer to your goal, and write them down the day before.

Then, spend about one or two hours each day working extensively on your action steps. After you have completed your action steps, congratulate yourself. You've just taken a huge step toward your goals! Place that small victory in your victory jar.

USE THE NEXT COUPLE OF PAGES TO COMPLETE THE EXERCISES

EXERCISE ONE

Use this area to write down some small victories that you made this week or the previous week.

_____

_____

_____

_____

_____

_____

_____

_____

_____

_____

_____

_____

_____

EXERCISE TWO

List the goals that you want to accomplish and the action steps needed to reach them.

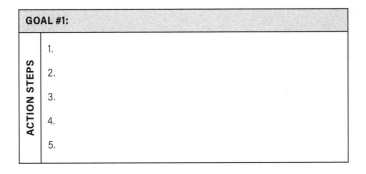

GOAL #1:

ACTION STEPS

1.
2.
3.
4.
5.

GOAL #2:

ACTION STEPS

1.
2.
3.
4.
5.

GOAL #3:

ACTION STEPS

1.
2.
3.
4.
5.

MINDSET IS EVERYTHING

I changed my mindset and it changed my life.

BRANDON ANDERSON @COVEREDWORLDWIDE

'm sure you've either heard this saying or seen someone rocking the T-shirt. Brandon, one of my good friends from college, started a T-shirt printing business and had this quote printed on a shirt. As soon as he shared an Instagram post promoting the shirt, I called him and told him I needed one of those shirts, and he sent me a couple.

Personally, I'm not too big on quotes because most times they can be overused and lose their value. But this particular quote is one I connect with on a personal level because when I finally changed my mindset, it indeed changed my life.

The way you process information can mean everything, from living life on someone else's terms or living life on your own terms, and I choose to live life on my own terms.

Training your mind to match your aspirations is vital to achieving the success you desire. Just think, have you ever witnessed a successful person always complaining with a negative attitude? I haven't. The most successful people I come across all possess one single quality.

They're positive about everything, even when things are not going their way; they seem to look for the good in every situation. That's because, although things may not go in their favor, they have accepted the lessons that life has given them, learned from them, and continued to move forward.

On season one, episode two of *Become Inspired*, I interviewed award-winning audio engineer Irko from Italy. He realized that New York was the hub for hip-hop at the time and bought a one-way ticket, with no plans on returning to Italy. At this time, Irko could barely speak English. I asked him if he ever had any doubts about making it in the industry, and his answer was no because he believed that the music was specifically created for him. Despite all of Irko's barriers and obstacles, he trained his mind that there wasn't anything he could not overcome.

Changing your mindset is a necessity for good things to start to happen in your life. Without it you'll remain stuck and frustrated. In season two of my docuseries, entrepreneur Deeja B., a successful businesswoman and hairstylist in the Atlanta metropolitan area, tells the story of when she graduated from cosmetology school and a stylist offered her a position at a shop in McDonough, Georgia, which is about forty minutes from Atlanta. Deeja refused at first because she had never heard of McDonough and thought the city was too slow paced and too country for her. It was when Deeja made the decision to move down to McDonough to learn what other stylists were doing that she began to grow in different areas and learn a variety of marketing tactics that she still uses for her business today.

If Deeja had refused to get out of her own way and not change her mindset, she would have missed out on building clientele and the opportunity to learn valuable skills for her business.

William King Hollis (season two, episode three) is a successful international motivational speaker who changed his mindset after a cracked vertebra ended his football career, leaving him depressed and on the verge of suicide. On the day William was thinking about ending his life, he was asked to speak to a group of kids who were headed in the wrong direction. It was there he recognized the opportunity he was being given: to share his life experiences with others so that they could avoid making decisions that could negatively affect their life. William changed his mindset from being depressed and pitiful because he could no longer play football, to being a positive teacher who served others.

Changing his mindset allowed William to make a smooth career change into the world of motivational speaking and fill the void left by not being able to play football. This catapulted William's speaking career, and he now speaks to more than three million kids worldwide.

Let me give you another example of how mindset is everything. This comes from Andrae Alexander, a successful musician and composer who, by the way, composed season two of *Become Inspired* in its entirety. Throughout Andrae's music career, he has added outstanding accolades to his resume, such as being assigned to the White House as a pianist, three Billboard awards, and an Image Award for the film *Detroit*, to name a few. One day Andrae's friend, who handles USC's job procurement, sent out a mass email with an opening for a lecturer in the music department at USC. The imposter syndrome immediately attacked Andrae's mind. Even with all his credentials, he still thought he wasn't successful enough to apply.

The idea of letting this opportunity slip away made him angry. Andrae applied for the position and is now a lecturer at USC. Just think, if Andrae had given in to that imposter syndrome, he would not have a job at USC and most likely would have given up other opportunities he thought he wasn't worthy of. The power of the mind can either propel you forward or hinder your personal and professional growth.

After I graduated from Columbus State University in 2007, I lived there for another four years before I packed up my bags and drove 3,000 miles away to Los Angeles. While living in Georgia, I became good friends with BK Jackson, who was also a communications major and always ahead of the curve on tech advancements. BK put together a presentation for instructors and students on the future of blogging. I know, I sound like a dinosaur, but 2005 was the early stages of Facebook as well as the birth of blogging, and it seemed as if no one knew where it was heading except BK. The department chair of the communications department was so impressed, he instructed BK to provide a template for the other departments.

We were always working on numerous passion projects together. About three years after we graduated, I worked for a local radio station as a radio personality, and BK started a video production business—shooting, editing, and producing content for clients. One day BK reached out to me about working together, so we had a meeting in his office where he basically sold me on how we could help each other. I signed the contract without hesitation. Back then, I was a novice on using camera equipment and editing software, so having someone who knew how to shoot and edit the content I wanted to create was a no-brainer for me, but we'll get back to this point later.

When we began to work together, we created a music countdown show, something similar to the late 90's BET music show *Hits from the Streets*, where I would be somewhere on location, like the annual Essence Music Festival that takes place every year in New Orleans, and interview people. These bits played between every other video. The show was so legit, we set up a meeting with a top-level programmer at a local CW television station in town, and he agreed to air the show as a paid-programming agreement.

I think it was something like thirty dollars per spot and they played at six a.m. and overnight, which was perfect because our target audience would get home from the club and watch our show.

Now let's go back to me being a novice on using camera equipment and editing software. While BK was like a blessing sent from heaven, it came back to haunt me when I moved out to Los Angeles on my own because I didn't have BK to shoot and edit for me. I couldn't afford to pay an editor or videographer here in Los Angeles, so I did the only thing I could at the time:

call BK to edit some content for me. I bought a camera on my own and started to play with it, but as far as learning editing software, I stayed away from it until I was forced to "boss up," as BK told me, or continue to miss opportunities to grow personally and professionally. To get to the next level, I needed to learn everything possible about production and develop the skills necessary to get me there. I would fly back to Atlanta every holiday, and on one of those holidays I bought a MacBook Pro and had a friend download the Final Cut X editing software to my Mac. I still have the MacBook with the editing software, and I use it to create the *Become Inspired* promotional video clips for social media.

It was a change in mindset that allowed me to go from being dependent on others to making things happen on my terms for myself.

Changing your mindset comes down to changing your perspective and training your mind to see things in a new light. As humans, we naturally lean toward a negative outlook about our hopes and dreams either because we think we lack a certain skill set or believe some external force keeps us from getting where we want to be. This is when you have to challenge your thoughts against the evidence. I know this sounds easier said than done, but when you take the time to meditate and prove that your current negative outlook is just a false reality, you'll begin to slowly change the way you think, and your path to success will start to become much clearer.

Where is your mindset today, and what's stopping you from growing and going further in your personal and professional life?

WEEK THREE EXERCISES

Let's focus on some exercises that will help you change the way you think as well as change your perspective.

Exercise One

A good exercise to start the change in mindset is to create a morning mindset routine. Set your alarm clock to wake up twenty minutes before you would normally get up; don't worry, you can do this exercise while you're still lying in bed. Make a mental list of everything you're looking forward to doing that day. This could be working on your business, delivering a presentation at work, meeting with your team, writing a new chapter in your book, or working on a new production set. The main thing is to start your day focusing on what makes you happy and gives you a feeling of accomplishment so you can keep taking small steps toward the life you desire.

Exercise Two

Listen to personal growth videos or audio books of your favorite public figures while getting ready for work and while driving to your destination. These positive messages fuel your motivation and put you in the right mindset to finish the day strong. I enjoy listening to Bishop TD Jakes, Les Brown, and Robert Kiyosaki. There are many personal growth videos on Instagram, so find someone you enjoy listening to and implement this exercise into your morning routine.

USE THE NEXT COUPLE OF PAGES TO COMPLETE THE EXERCISES

EXERCISE ONE

How did your mindset routine go this morning? What did you meditate on, and how did it impact your day on a positive level?

_____

_____

_____

_____

_____

_____

_____

_____

_____

_____

_____

_____

EXERCISE TWO

What motivational speaker do you enjoy listening to and why? How were you empowered today after listening to their message?

_____

_____

_____

_____

_____

_____

_____

_____

_____

_____

_____

_____

4

MAKE EVERY SECOND OF THE DAY COUNT

You should dedicate four-quarters
of your day to perfecting your craft.

TAAMU WUYA @TRAINERWUYAFITNESS

I was having a conversation with my good friend Taamu, whom I met in Los Angeles and connected with instantly since we're both creatives. He was telling me that he looks at his days in four quarters. His four quarters consist of working to pay bills, working on his craft, going on auditions, and meditating on the day. And then he said, "If I dedicate four-quarters of my day to perfecting my craft, excelling in greatness, then by the end of the day I know I will be fulfilled." I thought that was such a clever way of putting your daily routine into perspective to help alleviate the stress of working a job just to pay bills until your dream job comes knocking. I believe this way of thinking allows your mindset to make a shift from "Why me?" to "I have complete control over my destiny."

I know this is such a cliché, but we all have the same twenty-four hours in a day, so you have to be honest with yourself about how you use those hours. What time do you start your day? What time do you go to bed? How much time do you spend binge-watching Netflix shows? How much time do you spend scrolling on social media? These daily pleasurable activities can take up a great amount of your day, if not the entire day, but the good thing is that you have the power to change this. You can set your alarm clock to wake up earlier to get your day started. You have the power to control how much TV you watch and when you watch it. You can change your social media settings to alert you when you go over a daily quota.

I promise you, when you begin to break down your time spent on pleasurable activities, you'll find a lot more time to accomplish the goals you set for yourself.

Today, as I write these words, the world as we know it is on lockdown because of the global pandemic of COVID-19, and stay-at-home orders have been mandated in parts of America as well as across the world. Despite what's going on around me and being locked up in my home, I'm taking full advantage of the time to knock out some goals that I set for myself but never got around to accomplishing because of the busy world around me. I've been able to make use of my time to scratch things off my list and move to the next goal. I've been writing this book on and off for about a year now, and the pandemic has given me the extra time I need to finish it. I've put myself on a schedule to wake up at 5 a.m. and write for two to three hours a day until I complete the book. This is the time that I would not have had if the world opened back up today, so I'm using it to my advantage.

GET AN EARLY START

Take a minute to think about the successful people you admire and ask yourself if you think they're morning people. Of course they are; you don't even have to think twice about it. It's not a coincidence that successful people are early risers; it's a fact. When you rise two to three hours earlier than you normally would, that's two to three hours to get more things accomplished in the day. I was reading an article online, and it referred to maintaining your body's *circadian rhythm*, which means when you create good sleep habits, your internal clock cues your body to do different things at different times. Just using my sleep pattern as an example, every night around 9pm, no matter how hard I may try to stay up and finish watching a movie on Netflix, my eyes get dry and heavy, and I end up calling it a night and going to bed. My body is cued to go to bed at 9 p.m. and wake up at 5 a.m. without an alarm clock.

It's a proven fact that people who wake up earlier to get an early start have certain characteristics that night owls do not. People who get an early start tend to have a more positive outlook on life, are great problem solvers, are more organized, and are healthier mentally and physically. You will find that when you rise earlier, there will be a sense of accomplishment and an eagerness to get the rest of your day started.

To clarify, getting an early start does mean going to bed at a decent time to get at least eight to nine hours of sleep. Believe it or not, I've heard people say that if you want to be successful, there needs to be less sleep and a lot more grinding. I've even heard a public figure with a radio show say that three to four hours of sleep is enough. I think that's the most absurd thing I have ever heard. When the body is tired, the brain is tired, and when the brain is tired, productivity simply becomes busy work. Proper rest allows your body to heal and promotes healthy brain function. But don't take my word for it, try it for yourself and watch how your life begins to turn around for the better.

DEVELOP A ROUTINE

Creating a daily routine starts with getting an early start, but how are you spending the rest of your day? Creating a daily routine is essential in building productive habits over time. It took me a while to figure this out, but now I'm on a fixed schedule every day, and my productivity has increased substantially. I wake up at five every morning to work on my book, then I end my writing session at 7:30 a.m. Then, from 8 a.m. to 9 a.m., I get a good workout in with my trainer and head back to the house to shower and eat breakfast. From 10 a.m. to 12:30 p.m., I work on creating different Facebook ads for my series *Become Inspired*, post content to my page, respond to emails, work on my second project, and, if I have time, I'll clean my place. Then, from 1 to 6 p.m. I drive for Uber to make a little extra money to pay for my passion projects' expenses. This is my daily routine five days out of seven, but it keeps me on track to accomplish my goals.

Creating a system that works for you and following it each day is a great way to stay laser-focused while moving closer to your end goal. As Aristotle said, "We are what we repeatedly do. Excellence then is not an act, but a habit." By creating a successful routine, you are unconsciously building healthier habits to the point where missing one day of your routine makes you feel bad, making you want to get back on schedule. Every successful entrepreneur has a fixed schedule they rarely deviate from because of the productivity attached to it.

I know you may be asking: How can I get myself on a daily schedule with an eight to five that takes up nine hours of my day? Well, it starts with asking yourself how early are you willing to wake up so you can put an extra hour or two into your goals before work. Also, how are you spending your time between coming home from work and when you go to bed? You can spend two hours and end the night working on your goals. It's really about finding those small gaps of time in your schedule and implementing a fixed schedule to move closer to your goals.

It's also helpful to plan your schedule a day or even a week before to prevent getting lost in your to-do list. Eliminating as many decisions as possible for the next morning will give you the mental muscle and willpower you'll need for the entire day.

MAKE ROOM FOR WHAT MATTERS MOST

I've wasted so much time on things that were taking me away from my main focus. Living out here in Los Angeles, it's easy to get sidetracked if you're pursuing a career in the entertainment industry. Los Angeles is the mecca of entertainment, and you'll find yourself sucked into a completely different area of focus when your strategic baby steps aren't working out as expected and you can end up lost.

That's what happened to me as I was pursuing my radio broadcasting career. I really didn't know what direction to turn because what I've always thought I should be doing wasn't working. One day I was approached by a friend who thought highly of me and suggested I attend a meeting with her and team members of a network marketing company she was involved with. During this time of my life, I was more confused than ever about my true purpose, so I took her up on her offer and attended the meeting. This network marketing company brought in potential weekly recruits for the organization. As I sat through the pitch and history of the company, I still had no idea what this network marketing company really was, but I decided to hang in there because I was in desperate need of a career change.

After the meeting, I was introduced to the sponsor of the friend who'd invited me, and he invited me to yet another meeting. It wasn't until about four meetings in that I finally understood what this network marketing was all about. In short, network marketing is building a team and motivating your team to reach certain quotas by selling merchandise through a multi-marketing company. In this particular case it was Amway. For the different levels you reach within the company, you receive higher bonuses based on your team reaching quotas and recruitment. These meetings went on for about two months, and I did not want to say no to the invite because it would be a deciding factor on if they would recruit me. As I told you, I was desperate for anything that could put me in a position to be successful. They invited me to an annual conference held in Vegas, and of course I accepted and drove four hours with my wife for a two-day seminar. My wife thought I was crazy, but she tagged along because I was going to Vegas.

To make the long story short, about two weeks after attending the Vegas seminar, they decided they wanted to recruit me into the organization and presented me with their membership offer. I told them to give me some time to think about it. About a week later while attending another meeting, the sponsor asked the friend who invited me to rescind the offer because I was indecisive. I was shocked and disappointed because they presented themselves as an organization looking to help people find their way in the midst of being lost.

About a week later, I was thinking about how much time I wasted on something that really did not matter to me. I was more interested in being accepted into something that could fill the void left by my career in radio broadcasting. To be totally honest, I knew network marketing was a good choice if I decided to go that way, but deep down I knew that it wasn't the right choice for me. During the course of attending these meetings and conferences, I was missing opportunities to be involved in great projects as well as missing different press junkets and red carpet events I would normally cover for media outlets.

This experience taught me to always make room for what matters the most and get rid of what's unnecessary. You may have detoured off into something you have no interest in to fill a void. I'm here to tell you that void needs to be filled with what matters the most to you. Sometimes all you need is a moment to sit still for your purpose to find you. I talk about this more in the book. And let's be clear, many times those unnecessary elements in your life can be friends or family who are toxic, so finding a way to distance yourself from the drama will also make room for what matters most. When you find yourself focusing on the things that matter the most to you, you'll find more time than ever to do the things that make you happy.

WEEK FOUR EXERCISES

In this chapter, I discussed making room for the things that matter most, so let's use this week to make some changes to your schedule and get rid of activities or projects that are taking time away from the things that matter most to you.

Exercise One

Take some time this week and think about the things that matter most to you and write them down in the area provided on the next page. This could be your family, friends, career, professional or personal growth, or whatever makes you happy and that you enjoy doing. I want you to also think about the things that take up the most time and you do not enjoy doing, then write those down as well. Use this week to slowly cut back and eventually eliminate those things that take away your time, and focus more on the things that make you happy.

Exercise Two

Let's create a daily routine around what matters most to you. An hour or two before you go to bed, plan your daily routine for the week by writing out your schedule from the time you wake up to the time you go to bed. If you work eight or nine hours out of the day, that's fine, write down that block of time as well. Maybe you could steal thirty minutes of your one-hour lunch to work on goals. Be sure to also write out your routine for when you get home, and include the time you eat dinner. The point is to be as specific as possible so you can build the healthy habit of a successful routine. Follow this schedule for the week and make adjustments as needed. Don't get down if you find yourself off schedule, just make adjustments as needed to get back on course.

USE THE NEXT COUPLE OF PAGES TO COMPLETE THE EXERCISES

EXERCISE ONE

List all things that matter the most, then list the things that matter the least to you.

WHAT MATTERS THE MOST TO YOU AND MAKES YOU HAPPY?	WHAT THINGS MATTER THE LEAST TO YOU AND TAKE UP TOO MUCH TIME?
1.	1.
2.	2.
3.	3.
4.	4.
5.	5.
6.	6.
7.	7.
8.	8.
9.	9.
10.	10.

EXERCISE TWO

Take this time to plan your daily routine for the week, including the things that matter the most to you, into your schedule.

DATE	Monday
DATE	Tuesday
DATE	Wednesday
DATE	Thursday
DATE	Friday
DATE	Saturday
DATE	Sunday

GRATITUDE

Every No, I had to say Thank You.

EDWARD A. FARMER @EDWARDAFARMER

In season two, episode three, of *Become Inspired*, I spoke with author Edward A. Farmer about the process of finding a literary agent, which took him two years and ninety-five no's before receiving his yes on the ninety-sixth try. During the period of being rejected, Edward made a promise to himself to say "thank you" for every no he received because he knew that the agents telling him no were just not the right person for him. He trusted that God would get him to the right person, and he did just that. Edward talked about this not being easy, but he decided to have an attitude of gratitude for just the fact that the agents responded to him. This cultivation of gratitude will help get you through rejection and improve your satisfaction with life.

Learning to be grateful was definitely something I needed to work on, and I still have to remind myself from time to time when I hear too many no's. More often than not, we need a reminder to ourselves that our life is not as bad as we think, and others have it way worse than we do. I remember watching an interview of *The Breakfast Club* morning show on Power 105, and while normally I don't agree with Charlamagne's antics, this day he said something that I gave some thought to. Charlamagne said that it should be mandatory for everyone to attend a funeral once a year because death puts everything in perspective. I thought about that for a while, and Charlamagne may have a point.

We get so bogged down in our own bubble and self-pity, death brings everything that we ever complained about into perspective and cultivates an attitude of gratitude.

Learning to exchange self-pity for gratitude will improve your mental and physical health, as well as your overall satisfaction in life.

PRACTICE MINDFULNESS

If you don't believe in the power of meditation, I encourage you to really try it, whether it's waking up at the crack of dawn, lying in your bed at night before you fall asleep, or just learning to be still in your own place with all the electronics and computers off, in complete silence. My favorite thing is to wake up early without turning on the television and just being present in the moment. I think about how far I've come and the people and family who support me. For me, there's something about getting up that early in the morning that refreshes my spirit and energizes me to tackle and knock down my goals. And just so you know, I'm not sitting cross-legged on the floor with my eyes closed. I know we see that image a lot on television and social media, but I don't do that. I just sit on my couch or bed with my eyes open, taking the time to think or reminisce on good times with friends and family. Mindfulness is just about being present in the moment while learning to slow down from our busy world and take the time to experience our environment.

SPEND TIME WITH LOVED ONES

There is nothing like practicing gratitude than spending time with the people you love. Think about how happy you are around Thanksgiving and Christmas holidays, bonding with your family, playing games, eating dinner together, and watching the basketball games or movies as a family. To me, that has to be the most priceless experience I could ever have. Since I've moved to Los Angeles away from my family in Atlanta, I make it a priority to fly home for Christmas while visiting my dad in San Diego for Thanksgiving. Around that time of year, family is what I need to balance the everyday hustle and bustle.

During the Christmas holiday, I always take two weeks' vacation to rejuvenate my mind, body, and spirit. This prepares me mentally to take on the new year. That two weeks of relaxation is how I'm able to sustain my motivation throughout the year. Whatever spending time with loved ones means to you, by all means make it a priority and do it.

KEEP A GRATITUDE JOURNAL

Gratitude journals are known to increase positivity and self-esteem, reduce stress, and overall make you a happier you. I have to admit, practicing mindfulness works better for me, but I've heard great things from people who keep a gratitude journal. In fact, (shameless plug) I'm releasing a gratitude journal (*100 Days of Gratitude*) on Amazon and Barnes and Noble along with this book that is much different than a typical journal. The one-hundred-page journal I've created provides questions rather than blank pages to help shift your perspective, cultivate gratitude, and nurture positive emotions.

A couple of years ago, I had two journals I used to write in daily; at the time, it served as therapy for me. This is when I worked at CBS Radio and was really stressed about how I envisioned my career and how my career was playing out in reality. I would keep my journal handy, and at the end of every thought I would write something positive to lift my spirits for that day, but to also keep me motivated anytime I went back to read my journal.

You have to find out what works best for you. When you figure that out, you can move forward and protect yourself when tough times come your way. Look at these methods to stay grateful as your shield of protection from rejection, false hope, and stagnant dreams. Tough times will surely come, but if you equip yourself with gratitude, all those negative emotions bounce right off your shield, making it easier to move forward.

WEEK FIVE EXERCISES

Let's use this week to work on practicing mindfulness as well as learning to be grateful for the things you have.

Exercise One

I talked about how I practice mindfulness by waking up at the crack of dawn and sitting or lying in silence for about twenty minutes. That's my way of practicing mindfulness, but maybe you like to take walks or sit on your porch and be present in the moment. Do whatever works for you, but I want you to unplug from the realities and only reflect on the good things in your life and how far you've come. Do this three times this week for about twenty to thirty minutes, and experience the rejuvenation of your mind and spirit.

Exercise Two

Write down some things you are grateful for and why you're grateful for them. Also, write down some positive reasons why your challenges made you the person you are today. We often forget that with challenges comes growth, so what have you learned from the challenges in your life? If you would like to take the next step at cultivating gratitude daily, get my one-hundred-day gratitude journal, *100 Days of Gratitude*, on Amazon.

USE THE NEXT COUPLE OF PAGES TO COMPLETE THE EXERCISES

EXERCISE ONE

What did you learn about yourself from your mindfulness session? How did your mindfulness session put things in perspective for you?

_____

_____

_____

_____

_____

_____

_____

_____

_____

_____

_____

_____

_____

EXERCISE TWO

What are some things that you are grateful for and why? How have your challenges made you who you are today? How have you grown?

_____

_____

_____

_____

_____

_____

_____

_____

_____

_____

_____

_____

6

THE POWER IN
SELF-HELP BOOKS

Everything you need to know is in a book.

ANDRAE ALEXANDER @ANDRAEALEXANDER

Never take for granted the power of self-help books to enhance your life. I have a small bookshelf in my dining room that I add a new book to every other month. I just purchased Austin Miller's *Free Houses: How to Build Your Real Estate*, and it's a great book on buying houses with little to no money if you're looking to get into the real estate business. Not only is it a compelling read, but it gives me the confidence to think and act beyond my limitations.

That book was referred to me by my composer friend Andrae Alexander, who was featured on season two, episode four of *Become Inspired.* We were having a conversation over lunch; I told him I was looking to get into real estate but didn't have the capital. He asked me, "How do you know that?" I looked puzzled, and he explained to me he'd once thought the same thing and someone referred him to the book, which he purchased. Now he owns a four-unit quadplex he rents to tenants.

Self-help books are all about learning, applying, and taking continuous, swift action without having to ask or depend on someone else to give you the answers. Self-help books can be powerful, building a higher sense of confidence to take on goals that you typically wouldn't take on. Before I moved out to Los Angeles nine years ago, I purchased *No Excuses* by motivational speaker Bryan Tracy and read it within one week. It gave me the confidence I needed to get out of my comfort zone and relocate to Los Angeles to pursue my dreams. There is a chapter in the book that deals with how making a decision is the starting point on moving upward and onward toward being the best version of yourself. All major changes in life come after making a decision to do something different, and, for me, that chapter was enough to finalize my decision to relocate.

The best thing about self-help books are the real-life examples and methods used to achieve a desired goal. You have firsthand experience right in front of you as well as the strategies you can apply to help you achieve your goal.

SMASH THROUGH LIMITATIONS

People who put limits on how successful they can be are their own worst enemy. I've come across people who are beyond talented, but they've put limits on their success and are crippled by those limitations. Anytime you offer a solution, they reply with another problem and more excuses as to why they cannot move forward. I'm sure you've met or personally know someone with this negative mindset. The number-one reason people place limitations on how far they can go is nothing other than F.E.A.R., False Evidence Appearing Real. That's why starting small with self-help books can ease those fears because you've been provided a blueprint that exposes the truth to your FEAR.

CREATE PERSONAL PROJECTS THAT ROCKET YOUR GROWTH

Creating personal projects builds confidence to take on more things that you might normally be afraid to take on. Building confidence in yourself acts as a special superpower, making you feel invincible, as if nothing is too big for you. And, in order to keep the invincibility going, you'll need to continue to do things that feed your confidence or those superpowers will eventually wear off. It's just like being inspired by someone or something on television: the inspiration stays with you for a day or two, but if you don't put that inspiration into action, it begins to fade slowly until it's gone.

While creating the *Become Inspired* series, I learned so much about the process of storytelling and the different processes of putting a documentary series together. I really felt myself growing as I was learning new things and was eager to learn even more, so I took it a step further and learned about Facebook ads. Since this project is an indie production, I knew that I was going to need to reach thousands and thousands of people on social media through marketing with Facebook ads. I have to admit this wasn't something I had great enthusiasm for, but I knew that to get to new levels I was going to have to become a new version of myself. As I was taking the courses online, I began to gain a sense of confidence in what I was doing and—again—had great enthusiasm to learn more. Now I'm running Facebook ads for season two, and every morning I check my performance data in Facebook business manager to get an idea of how well or how poorly my ad is doing and make adjustments according to the data.

Building confidence by taking on personal projects is the key to personal and professional development. When you begin to feel good about who you're becoming, you'll not only have the desire to want to do even more, but you'll have the desire to push past all those limitations you set for yourself.

As you focus on working toward your goals, you'll gain wisdom as well as experience, which will increase your confidence even more.

WEEK SIX EXERCISES

This week it's all about finding power in self-help books, as well as growing your confidence by working toward your goals.

Exercise One

Use this week to find a great self-help book related specifically to your dreams and goals. If you already have one on the bookshelf but haven't had time to crack it open, find time this week to read a couple of chapters. If you need to order your book and have to wait a couple of days, that's fine. Use Google to find self-help articles on the subject related to your dreams and indulge yourself in those articles until your book arrives. Learning new things and gaining insight empowers you to take step after step until you've reached your goal.

Exercise Two

Dedicate some time to working on a personal project you've always wanted to start but keep talking yourself out of, for whatever reason. Most times it's the fear of thinking you're not capable of completing the project. It could be that you've always wanted to write a book, a script, or maybe start a podcast. Use what you've learned in exercise one and apply those same methods as your starting point. The purpose of this exercise is to slowly build your confidence to go even further.

USE THE NEXT COUPLE OF PAGES TO COMPLETE THE EXERCISES

EXERCISE ONE

What are some new things that you've learned after indulging yourself with self-help books and articles? How has what you learned empowered you to move forward?

_____

_____

_____

_____

_____

_____

_____

_____

_____

_____

_____

_____

EXERCISE TWO

With the new information you've learned, what have you done this week to move forward? What's the next step for you?

_____

_____

_____

_____

_____

_____

_____

_____

_____

_____

_____

_____

_____

_____

7

MASTERING THE ART OF PATIENCE

Patience is bitter, but its fruit is sweet.

UNKNOWN

astering the art of patience is probably one of the most difficult things to do because our natural instinct is to want something when we want it. Living in the era of social media and advanced technology where instant gratification has become the new norm doesn't make patience any easier. While writing this chapter, I learned some history on the word *patience*. The word *patience* is derived from the Latin word *pati* which means "to suffer, to endure, or to bear," which of course makes perfect sense. I then researched the meaning of "patience is a virtue." I know we've heard that cliché over and over, but what does it mean? Let me explain. A virtue is a behavior showing high moral standards and is valued as a foundation of principle and good moral being. Having

patience means that you have mastered a personal character-
istic that others have failed to master and therefore positions
you to see the big picture in life instead of the small details.

My friend Andrae Alexander had a perfect analogy when I
asked him if he could share one piece of advice. Simply put, he
said, "Play your role. Start off in the kitchen chopping vegetables while the main chef is doing his gig. Soon enough, you'll
go from chopping vegetables to getting bigger and better and
better." Mastering the art of patience allows you to see beyond
the present moment and understand the importance of growing into your craft.

We all have these big dreams of being the best and getting to
new levels in life and you will, but it takes patience to get there.

Author Edward A. Farmer, who is a guest on episode three of
season two, also had an interesting revelation that he discov-
ered about his fifteen-year journey to becoming an author. He
said, "If I had reached a level of success one year before, two
years before, or anywhere earlier in the journey, I wouldn't
be where I am now because I was not prepared." Learning to
develop patience is the key component in capitalizing on an
opportunity that you've been preparing for.

COMPARISON IS THE THIEF OF JOY

Oftentimes the ability to be patient is blocked by a trait that is
self-destructing and demoralizes how we feel about ourselves
while also questioning our ability to perform at a high level.
Comparing yourself to others is the quickest way to sabotage
your dreams, your career, and your happiness. I have to admit,

I found myself guilty of doing this about two years after my move to Los Angeles. I was working for CBS radio at the time, and it seemed that no matter how hard I worked, I was always passed up and never would get an opportunity to prove myself. So after a long, stressful day, I would relax on the couch and pass the time by scrolling on social media. While scrolling, I would see some of my peers who were also in the same industry but thriving. Their social media posts focused on accepting a promotion, getting hired by a better company, or just getting more opportunities. That left me envious because I felt I deserved to be in their position but wasn't.

These comparisons eventually became a habit that was causing the destruction of my happiness, and I knew I needed to make a change. I vowed that I would never compare my success to the success of others again because my journey is different from their journey. I really started to conceptualize that life will take us all on different paths to get to our destination, and reaching my moment of success will be different than my peers' moments of success. When I was able to put that into perspective and truly understand it, was when I was able to let go of the comparison trait and focus on my journey, I became filled with a sense of peace and greater motivation.

In season one episode three, executive producer Noor Wahba of the Nick Cannon morning show on Power 106 in Los Angeles said this on what she learned from her journey in radio: "You know it's so hard when you see other people getting this job and getting that job, especially if you guys started at the same time, but I kept reminding myself that no, that's their journey and this is mine. All these struggles are going to be sweeter once I get to the top."

I believe that when you have reached the pinnacle of your struggle and are ready to give up is when God sends the clarity you need to see the struggle from a different perspective. He will remind you of past struggles you faced and were able to overcome. This light of perspective hits everyone at different times in their journey, and if we miss it the first time, it circles back again until we're able to see it clearly.

Author Edward A. Farmer (season two, episode two) briefly talked about being hit by that light of perspective and looking back at the struggles he faced as a poor child growing up in Memphis, Tennessee. "I've been through so much; this isn't that hard, I've been through worse. Being hungry at night and not having food, those are struggles that are worse than what I'm going through. And it was during those times where I would reflect back on, I've been taught the skills I need to get through this, how did I get through that tough childhood, and then once I remembered those lessons, I applied it to what I was going through."

Comparison is the gateway to self-doubt, depression, jealousy, and the destruction of your own happiness. In order to fight off this negative trait, you have to believe you're on the right track and you're on your own unique path to building a life and career that you're proud of.

WEEK SEVEN EXERCISES

Let's practice some ways to improve your patience. Below, I've put together a couple of exercises to improve your patience that I would like for you to implement into your daily schedule.

Exercise One

Learn to embrace the uncomfortable. I've learned from personal experience that when you embrace the comfort of being uncomfortable, we begin to cultivate a little more patience. So be mindful this week of the things that make you uncomfortable and embrace them.

Exercise Two

Change your self-hating narrative. All those times while writing in my journal, I always ended with a positive mantra that I would say to myself. "I got this, and I will never give up." This gave me the motivation I needed to carry me through the next day. I want you to read the mantra below and try to remember this and say it every morning before you start your day.

"I'm on the right track and my own unique path to building a life and career I love and that I'm proud of. I am not behind. I'm exactly where I need to be, learning and growing all the time."

USE THE NEXT COUPLE OF PAGES TO COMPLETE THE EXERCISES

EXERCISE ONE

What are some things that made you uncomfortable this week, and how did you embrace them?

_____

_____

_____

_____

_____

_____

_____

_____

_____

_____

_____

_____

_____

_____

EXERCISE TWO

After changing your self-hating narrative and verbalizing your mantra every morning, describe how your week turned out.

_____

_____

_____

_____

_____

_____

_____

_____

_____

_____

_____

_____

_____

_____

8

CHANGING YOUR SELF-TALK: POSITIVE AFFIRMATIONS

You are what you believe.

UNKNOWN

Never underestimate the power of positive self-talk. It can make the difference between someone who is accomplished and someone who finds themselves at a complete standstill, unable to accomplish any of their goals. Whether you say it aloud or in your head, self-talk plays a role in what you think about yourself, which affects how you feel about yourself, and how you feel about yourself affects how you behave. Can you think of a situation that led to negative self-talk? How did you behave and what was the outcome? Now, can you think of a situation that led to positive self-talk for you? How did you behave and what was the outcome? I'm sure there was a better outcome from the positive self-talk than from the negative self-talk.

IFBB (International Federation of BodyBuilding & Fitness) pro and friend Christina Bryant, whom I mentioned in the first chapter, wrote on her Facebook profile that she started a sticky-note challenge where she writes down positive affirmations and places them around her every day to love on herself while speaking positivity into the atmosphere. This is actually a great habit to develop and not only reprograms your self-conscious thought process, but also manifests your desires. I think the most important thing about writing these affirmations on a sticky note rather than in a journal is that you're forced to see the sticky note wherever you place it, and you're intentionally rereading them in order to manifest your desires. However, if a journal works for you, go ahead and stick with that.

I mentioned in the last chapter how I relieved stress by journaling daily while working at the radio station, but no matter how difficult that day was, I always ended the journal entry with a positive affirmation that helped reprogram my thought process.

Most, if not all, successful people practice some type of positive self-talk. Every guest featured in seasons one and two of *Become Inspired* mentioned a situation where they had to practice positive self-talk to build the confidence they needed to accomplish their goals.

Motivational speaker William King Hollis said, "When nobody would tell me anything great about myself, I would tell myself. And in this world they call it selfish, arrogant, cocky, but I say where we're from, when we speak to ourselves it's because we're the only person who ever told us that we could be something, the only person that saw something in us. So, if the world won't tell me I'm great, only I can tell me I'm great."

Positive self-talk can help you get from thinking you can do something to knowing you can do something, and it all starts with the reprogramming of your inner thoughts. When you hear that little voice in your head saying, *You can't do this*, respond out loud with, "I can do this," and repeat that phrase until your inner voice is silenced.

MONITOR THE NEGATIVE SELF-TALK OF PEOPLE AROUND YOU

This may be harder than it sounds because most of us are forced to be around negative people for eight hours of our day whether it's at work, or with family and friends. We can love our family and friends but find it hard to be in their space when they're being negative. There's nothing worse than going to work and politely greeting everyone and one person responds with something negative as a means to start up a conversation that you have no use for. I used to work with someone like that, and I was forced to avoid them at all costs because I couldn't handle their negative energy pulling me down and draining me emotionally. Who could? I was reading an article on entrepreneur.com on how to deal with a negative person, and one of the techniques they suggested is called *appreciative inquiry*, which is the process of answering questions to help the person gain a more positive outlook. So, if you're engaged in a conversation with someone who's complaining, take charge of the conversation by asking them questions that focus on the positive aspects of their experiences.

Jim Rome said it best: you are the average of the five people you spend the most time with, so if they're always negative and you're absorbing that energy, then guess what, that negativity has rubbed off on you. Negativity is contagious, and if you don't protect your mindset, you can easily fall victim to seeing the bad in everything."

SURROUND YOURSELF WITH POSITIVE PEOPLE

Positive people are the only people I hang around, and if you ask any other successful person, they'll tell you the same thing. Just like there's something about hanging around negative people and absorbing that energy, there's also something good about hanging around positive people and feeding off all of that positivity.

Andrae Alexander said something during his interview on the power of relationships and hanging with successful people that really resonated with me: "Your circle is literally the thing. So when people ask how am I successful, you can look around at my friends who are successful, I like the way they think, if I like the way you think and like you as a person and now you happen to be successful, so when something happens, you bring me in and I bring you in and we work together and it's a synergy."

When we surround ourselves with positive people, we clear away the negativity around us and create more room to welcome nurturing and renewing energy. I've also found that for myself, being in an environment and attending an event that has so much positivity and inspiration fosters better conditions to do better and be better in life. For instance, I was invited to an event by a very successful friend who has her own PR firm and organized a private screening for one of her clients, a filmmaker. This was maybe a year and a half before I created my series *Become Inspired*, but I was so inspired at the time that I was filled with a desire to grow as a producer and filmmaker. Fast-forward to two years later, and I've directed and produced my own documentary series, which is on Amazon.

Listening to the stories of determination and perseverance from Edward A. Farmer and Andrae Alexander, both published authors, gave me the energy I needed to complete this book you're reading now. Never take for granted what being in the presence of a positive person can do for your life.

WEEK EIGHT EXERCISES

This week, let's work on ways you can practice replacing negative self-talk with positive self-talk and speaking daily affirmations.

Exercise One

Identify the negative thoughts. These are thoughts that start or end with *I can't ... I will never ... This is not fair ... Why me?* Take some time this week and identify those thoughts and write them down.

1. Create a list.

Create a list of facts that do not support the negative thought. For instance, if your negative thought is, *I can never lose this weight,* begin to think about specific facts that prove this negative thought is wrong, such as, *I had a healthy breakfast this morning,* or *I worked out for thirty minutes after work.* Write as many of these specific things down and move to the next negative thought from step one.

2. Create a new positive thought.

Now let's create a new positive thought by adding, *I am* at the beginning of the sentence. Using the weight-loss example from above, start the sentence with an *I am* statement: *I am healthy. I am confident. I am in control.* Write these positive thoughts down under or next to the negative thought, and say them every time that negative thought crosses your mind. This repetition reprograms your mind, and if done efficiently, these positive thoughts can empower you and change your life.

USE THE NEXT COUPLE OF PAGES TO COMPLETE THE EXERCISES

EXERCISE ONE

Use the table to write down a list of facts that do not support the negative thought, then write a positive thought on the other side of the table, placing "I am" at the beginning of the sentence.

NEGATIVE THOUGHT:	
Facts that do not support negative thought.	*Write down a new positive thought.*
1.	1.
2.	2.
3.	3.
4.	4.
5.	5.

9

VISUALIZE YOURSELF SUCCEEDING

If you can imagine it,
you can achieve it.

UNKNOWN

Throughout my life, I've had a habit of visualizing myself succeeding regardless of what I was pursuing at the time. I always envisioned myself being the best and being recognized for it. This may sound silly to some, but the power of positive visualization and seeing yourself succeed long before it happens becomes a pivotal part of your success.

I have pictured myself several times in attendance at the Dolby Theatre in Los Angeles for the Oscars, anxiously waiting for my name to be called for Best Short Film, or Best Documentary Short, or even Best Director, and walking up to the stage, teary-eyed to deliver a short, empowering speech. I see it right now as I'm typing this, and it's as real as if it already happened and I'm reflecting on a nostalgic moment. While in production for season two of *Become Inspired*, I knew I wanted to have a private screening for close family, friends, and industry people, so I would visualize daily every detail of the event, from the venue to taking pictures in front of the backdrop to hosting a Q & A after the screening. I had it all planned out in my head, and it was perfect! On the day of the screening everything I had visualized was exactly as I'd seen it, if not better, on that night.

So, believe me when I tell you there is true power in envisioning yourself achieving your dreams and making your dream a reality. Before I heard others speak about how they visualized their success, I used to think that it was just something I did because I thought differently. There is a saying: "If you can imagine it, you can achieve it."

While interviewing guests for the series, they often reflect on a time when they envisioned themselves achieving a particular goal that later became a reality.

IFBB Pro Christina Bryant shared with me the time she envisioned herself taking home first place in the bodybuilding competition, and guess what, it became a reality.

"You might not see what you're looking at, but if you can envision yourself in that moment, in that spot, I still remember in the gym getting ready for nationals to go up for my pro card, I saw myself standing in that center box and not moving. And the judge is saying, 'Your new IFBB pro is Christina Bryant.' I envisioned that for myself and did everything I needed to be prepared for that moment."

During an Instagram Live with entrepreneur Deeja B, she spoke about how she envisioned her success and said that it was so clear, as if she had already lived it. The truth is, if you can't picture yourself achieving a goal, chances are you won't. Start thinking about your personal goals and spend ten to fifteen minutes picturing yourself achieving them, and watch your dreams come to reality.

THE POWER OF VISION BOARDS

If you have trouble visualizing your success, try using a vision board to display what you want out of life, and put it in a place where you'll see it often. This will help you to internalize what's displayed on your vision board, creating a more vivid vision of your ideal life.

Since I normally visualize my success from my imagination, I had never created a vision board until last year. I thought it would be fun to do something different; plus, I wanted to experience it for myself. People talk about planning vision board parties within the first three weeks of the new year. I have my vision board sitting in my bedroom on the floor at the end of the bed so I get to see it every morning when I get out of bed.

And from my experience, the vision board makes my vision that much clearer, creating an emotional connection that keeps me motivated and focused on bringing these desires to reality. Let's be clear, you'll need to do something each day to move closer to your goal, and it will take more than just visualizing; you actually have to put in the work. There is a scripture in the Bible that reads: "Faith without works is dead." Don't expect a change in your life if you don't put in the work.

Actress and Director Christina Cooper, who I spoke briefly about in the first chapter, said this about her moment on envisioning herself on the Emmys red carpet: "I'm a strong believer in manifesting stuff and that you speak it into existence. I even make vision boards. I cut out a picture of myself and placed it on an Emmy carpet, and I walked the Emmys red carpet last year twice."

Creating a vision board and placing it somewhere you're forced to see it every day works miracles within your mind that help make the dream possible to achieve. And while most people create their vision boards at the beginning of the year, you can get started right now and begin what's called the Law of Attraction, manifesting all your dreams and goals.

TALK ABOUT YOUR DREAMS

There's some connection between voicing your dreams out into the universe and witnessing everything you spoke about materializing in reality. Every chance I have, I talk to like-minded individuals and share my goals and dreams with them as a way for them to keep me accountable for following through on those dreams. It's a reverse psychology I use on myself because I want to be known as a man of my word, and I never want to let down the people I admire.

When you tell like-minded individuals your goals and dreams, it grants them permission to follow up with conversations and hold you accountable. Think about the last time you told someone you were going to do something and you didn't do it, then a couple of days or weeks went by and they followed up with you about it. How did that make you feel? It makes me feel like a complete phony. All talk, no action.

While it's helpful to talk about your dreams to like-minded individuals, remember not to share those same aspirations with friends, family, or colleagues who have the complete opposite aspirations for themselves and for you. Oftentimes the people closest to us, who claim to have our best interest at heart, will crush a dream and project their fears onto us. Although they may have good intentions, their discouraging remarks could be too damaging to recover from.

While I was in the process of transitioning to Los Angeles, I kept my plan to relocate a secret from my family and even my partner at the time, who is now my wife. I had already made my mind up and had begun the process of looking for apartments and setting up an employee transfer request to a store in Los Angeles. At the time I was working part-time at Home Depot, and of course Home Depot has stores all over the country, so it was a no-brainer that this was the right decision. About two months before my departure, I finally told my family and my partner and was prepared to hear their fears for me moving alone to a big city, but I was already in too deep to turn back.

A couple of weeks before the move, my family began to support my decision because they realized that there was no turning back for me and that I needed to do this for myself. If I decided to share my dream with them during the preliminary stage, all those fears they likely would have projected onto me would probably have killed my dream of moving to Los Angeles. So keep your dreams and plans to yourself unless you decide to share it with someone who will encourage you to follow through from the start.

Another benefit to sharing your dreams with like-minded individuals is unexpectedly receiving help from those who not only want to cheer you on but want to help you get there. Several times, sharing my vision with someone who I think will encourage me to go for it has led to them helping me get there. Around this time last year, I had just launched my series *Become Inspired* on Amazon, and I wanted to write a book about staying inspired throughout the journey but didn't have a clue on how to start.

One day I was having a meeting with one of my writer friends, Barak, who I speak about in the acknowledgments, and told him about the idea I had for writing this book. He thought my idea was a good one and offered to help me create an outline to get started. It wasn't until Barak helped me create the outline that I was able to see the vision for the book with clarity. By sharing your vision with those who will root for you from the start, you could be enlisting the help you need to reach your end goal.

THE LAW OF ATTRACTION

Visualizing and talking to others about your dreams are just two ways of using the Law of Attraction. What you constantly think about, believe strongly about, and feel intensely about, you will bring about. It's that simple. Our words and thoughts are made up of big balls of energy that will either attract positivity or negativity, which is why speaking and believing positivity ensures the manifestation of our dreams. Whatever you give your focus, energy, and attention to, you'll eventually attract into your life.

In 2019, my wife, Monica, was determined to start a transportation business for the elderly, taking them to and from medical appointments, hospital discharges, and medication pickups. Every day she would come home from her nine-to-five with another idea for the company, and then one day she came to me with great enthusiasm. She wanted to name her business MJ Reliable Transportation using the letters *M* and *J* after the first initial in both her name as well as her business partner's name. She was ecstatic. Over the next couple of weeks, she came up with an idea for the logo then hired a graphic designer and applied to get the business license as well as taking all the certifications needed for the business.

That's all my wife thought about last year: starting a business, which then manifested in 2020. Monica and her business partner, Jasmine, purchased their first van at the beginning of the year, then hired someone to wrap the van in the company's brand and are now legitimate entrepreneurs in the transportation business. Monica and Jasmine committed their focus to becoming entrepreneurs ,and it materialized into reality.

My best friend used the Law of Attraction to pursue his dream of becoming a basketball coach. In college, TJ was a true fan of the game of basketball and loved coaching others. While we were out doing fun things that college kids do, TJ volunteered to help train the school's women's basketball team and focused on giving all of his time to coaching and training those basketball players. We used to give TJ a hard time and tease him, but he didn't care; he was on a mission to pursue his true purpose. About a year later, TJ got the last laugh when he was hired by the head coach to be the new assistant coach for the team. TJ now coaches college basketball for the University of Baltimore, Maryland. TJ gave his dream the attention it needed in his thoughts, words, and actions, which manifested and materialized into reality.

What are you constantly thinking about and giving your attention to? Are you attracting positive or negative events into your life? Ask yourself these questions, then make some changes based on your thoughts, words, and actions.

WEEK NINE EXERCISES

This week's exercises will be focused on visualizing yourself succeeding.

Exercise One

Create a vision board around your list of goals that you'd like to achieve this year. First, take a minute to write out those goals, then find some magazines (you can find them for a dollar at any thrift store) and a poster board from the dollar store. Next, you're going to select pictures that represent your goals and inspire you. When you have gathered your images, paste your pictures to the board.

It's also helpful to look for affirmation words in the magazines to paste to the board. If you've already created a vision board this year, feel free to create another one, or you can move on to exercise two.

Exercise Two

Start up a conversation with a like-minded friend, family member, or colleague about your goals. Share with them what you'd like to accomplish and what you're working toward. They may offer to help you in some way, which is great, but if they don't, there's no need to feel discouraged, since the main purpose of the exercise is to keep you accountable and encourage you to follow through on your goals.

USE THE NEXT COUPLE OF PAGES TO COMPLETE THE EXERCISES

EXERCISE ONE

Visualize your goal as if it already happened. Then in detail, describe the things that you see as well as the recognition you receive for your accomplishments.

_____

_____

_____

_____

_____

_____

_____

_____

_____

_____

_____

_____

EXERCISE TWO

Who did you share your goals with, and what good thing came out of the conversation?

_____

_____

_____

_____

_____

_____

_____

_____

_____

_____

_____

_____

_____

_____

10

STUDY INSPIRING PEOPLE

What is most personal is most universal.

UNKNOWN

There is something powerful about studying people you admire. It's one of my favorite weekly things to do where I either read someone's biography online, watch a documentary biopic, or purchase a memoir. Watching or reading about someone's journey to overcome the obstacles that stood in their way has to be one of the most inspirational ways to keep you moving closer to your dreams.

That was my purpose when I was creating the *Become Inspired* series; I knew what these stories could do for someone experiencing a major setback or who feels that no matter what they do, they just can't seem to get over the hump and are on the verge of giving up. It provides a sense of hope to see those who've gone through similar obstacles in life come out on top. What is most personal is most universal, which is why watching the success stories of others restores our hope and sparks our inspiration.

I often watch interviews from some of the black directors I admire, such as Tyler Perry, Issa Rae, Ava DuVernay, Barry Jenkins, Jordan Peele, and Ryan Coogler, to name a few. From each interview about their journey, I have learned something new that fuels my inspiration and helps me put obstacles into perspective. This allows me to not only cherish the journey but to also embrace the hardships that come with it because those hardships help me grow in areas I need to grow, preparing me for the new levels I plan to reach. I did the same thing when I was pursuing a career in radio broadcasting, watching interviews of Atlanta radio personalities like Frank Ski, Ryan Cameron, the legendary Larry King, Ryan Seacrest, and even Howard Stern. When watching these interviews, my goal wasn't to focus on their success, per se, but to focus on the hardships that made them successful and use that to help pivot my perspective from a negative mindset about my struggles into a positive mindset.

The advantage of studying those you admire is that you gain experience through other people's stories and can avoid making the same mistakes they did, shortening your journey.

Entrepreneur and hairstylist Deeja B shared how she studied other beauticians while moving to a new shop on the other side of town, noticing what they were doing and what they were not doing. "I decided to go ahead and start doing hair in McDonough, Georgia, and a lot of the young ladies in the hair salon had been there for a couple of years and they didn't have a lot of clientele and [did not] experience a lot of growth while they were there. I started to study the things they were doing and the things they were not doing, and one of the young ladies taught me how to post on Craigslist. Everyone in the shop was posting on Craigslist, but they were only posting one picture. I found out that Craigslist at the time allowed you to post thirty-four pictures, so I began posting all thirty-four pictures and that's when I learned that people want to see pictures of your work." By studying the other beauticians, Deeja was able to shorten her learning curve and double her clientele.

WHY THE JOURNEY IS MORE IMPORTANT THAN THE DESTINATION

Life is a series of small moments, and the goal is not to acquire things but rather to learn how to focus on and enjoy the process of success. This was really hard for me to grasp and accept because all I wanted was to accomplish the goal at hand; I couldn't care less about what was happening in between. If I felt like the journey was taking longer than I expected, I would get frustrated and my happiness was delayed because I failed to reach my goal at a certain time.

It wasn't until four years ago, when I was laid off from the radio station, that I really understood the importance of everything I'd endured and that all the skills I'd acquired along the way would work in my favor for my next endeavor. I realized that I was equipped to do so many other things because of those years spent sharpening the tools in my tool belt. It was then that I reflected on the idea of enjoying the process of success, and I finally understood what that meant.

The valuable things that go unnoticed while on the journey are the new habits being formed and the incredible amount of experience gained. With all the distractions around us and the noise from our inner thoughts, the mind becomes clouded with disappointment and frustration, leaving us blind to our true purpose. But by focusing on and learning to enjoy the journey, you'll begin to see beyond the reality and discover what fulfills you the most.

EMBRACE THE UNCERTAINTY

Uncertainty is probably our most difficult obstacle to overcome. But it's uncertainty that gives room for possibilities to open up. Think about a time when your back was against the wall and you were uncertain about your future, but somehow you were able to get past your emotions, figure it out, and recognize a better opportunity when it came along. That's because that feeling of uncertainty allows us to reevaluate the past and make new choices. Uncertainty presents opportunities to create a compelling future based on new information. It's mind-boggling how uncertainty works in our favor if we learn to embrace it and allow a change in our perspective. Our most ambitious plans emerge through the obscuring veil of uncertainty.

Andrae Alexander spoke about how he embraced being uncomfortable after moving to Los Angeles and having to give up the last four hundred dollars in his pocket for rent, but something amazing happened. "I got to Los Angeles March 1, 2009, and I was supposed to stay with some friends on the couch for free. March 1, two hours later, they said, 'Dre, she can't pay her half of the rent … can you pay half of the rent?' I only had four-hundred-something dollars in my pocket after driving from Maryland all the way here, and it cost four-hundred-something dollars to get here. I could have either driven home or been in Los Angeles, and I had the thought … I guess I'm going to die here in Los Angeles. I gave her the money and on March 2, 2009, I checked Craigslist and I saw a post looking for an African American jazz pianist. I sent in a picture and by March 3, I was in a Kanye West video.

Andrae knew that having no money in his pocket and being two thousand miles from home was going to put him in an uncomfortable situation financially, but he embraced the uncertainty and found a new opportunity that launched his music career in Los Angeles.

Entrepreneur Deeja B also went through a point in life when she was faced with uncertainty in her future. Deeja was in a tough situation after she left her corporate job to pursue her dream of becoming a cosmetologist. She wasn't sure how she was going to survive financially while raising a daughter and trying to pay her mortgage and car loan. This is when an opportunity kicked in after she reevaluated the situation. "I could not successfully complete my plan and my dreams with this mortgage, so I tried going to different places to get an apartment to rent my house out, but I couldn't afford to live anywhere, literally. I lived off of a $326 unemployment check, so I made a call to my father and said, "This is what I want to do." He asked me if I was sure … and I said again, "This is what I want to do!" So I rented my house out and I moved in with my father while I completed hair school.

Deeja realized that in order for her plan to work, she needed to embrace the uncertainty and figure out a way to do both.

This allowed her to reevaluate the situation and make the right choice based on the new information. The seeds of opportunity lie in the unexpected and, while embracing the uncertainty, we prevail.

DO MORE OF WHAT FUELS YOU

These were the words said to me by my good friend BK, who I talked about in chapter three. I'll never forget those words after having a conversation on how energized I felt after launching my webisode in 2014. I was so excited and moved by this because, as I mentioned earlier, those first couple of years after arriving in Los Angeles were pretty tough and mentally draining for me. I worked at Home Depot for the first seven hours of the day, then headed over to the radio station for another six- or seven-hour shift. I was not only exhausted, I was missing that connection from doing the things that fueled me, and I felt no inspiration. I've always had a passion for creating meaningful content, even before I realized it, but that's when I decided to do it, and the very first piece of content I created after moving to Los Angeles was the hip-hop webisode "Oh Yeah We Talk." I would invite three of my colleagues from the radio station, and we'd discuss the trending topics of the week.

This brought me back to doing the things that fueled my inspiration, and I finally felt like myself again after four years of being in Los Angeles. This one thing sparked my inspiration to create, which eventually led me to develop *Become Inspired*. When you begin to do the things you love, you get into the flow of losing yourself in what you're doing and find it easier to stay motivated to keep the inspiration flowing.

While you're doing all the things that fuel you, there is very little time to get bogged down in what really doesn't matter. You'll find that if you allow yourself to be driven by your passions, new opportunities are always waiting. I think Oprah said it best: "Know what sparks the light in you, then use that to illuminate the world."

WEEK TEN EXERCISES

This week, let's focus on sparking your inspiration and doing an exercise that will fuel your motivation. Be sure to apply these activities into your daily schedule, and watch how your inspiration ignites.

Exercise One

Study inspiring people. Take this week to really study someone you admire, whether personally or professionally, by watching a recent interview or documentary and learning new details about them, reading one of their books, or maybe just following them on social media and taking a look at their profile to see if they have a website to direct you to and read their bio. This will begin your inspiration process.

Exercise Two

Do more of what fuels you. Conduct a personal audit of what you love to do. Use the table on the next page and list everything you're good at, whether you like doing it or not, in the first column. In the second column, list all the things you don't enjoy doing; this could include the responsibilities at your job or everyday tasks. And lastly, in the third column, list all your passions. Think about the things you could do for hours without realizing how much time has passed. This will allow you to discover what fuels you and to focus on these things in your personal and professional life.

EXERCISE ONE

What did you find interesting from studying the person you admire?

_____

_____

_____

_____

_____

_____

_____

_____

_____

_____

_____

_____

_____

_____

EXERCISE TWO

Use the table below to conduct a personal audit on your likes and dislikes.

WHAT ARE YOU GOOD AT?	WHAT DO YOU HATE DOING?	WHAT DO YOU LOVE TO DO?
1.	1.	1.
2.	2.	2.
3.	3.	3.
4.	4.	4.
5.	5.	5.
6.	6.	6.
7.	7.	7.
8.	8.	8.
9.	9.	9.
10.	10.	10.

CONNECTING YOURSELF SPIRITUALLY

Spiritual practice is key to a meaningful life.

OPRAH WINFREY

We're all working toward something, or maybe we haven't started but we've been meaning to get around to it … one of these days. Inspiration can be difficult to keep alive, especially when dealing with the realities of life. Some of us could be dealing with the death of a close family member or friend, some with financial hardships because of COVID-19, and others may be battling some form of depression, in which case I suggest you seek professional help. I've learned to tell myself that nothing good or bad lasts forever, and that this, too, shall pass. I know this is easier said than done, but it's an effective way to push through the most difficult times.

While navigating the roller coaster of highs and lows of my journey, I have to honestly say that if it weren't for my spiritual belief and religion, I wouldn't have been able to get through, much less be where I am today. I thought it would be best to share my thoughts on religion here in the last chapter because I realize some of you may not practice it and may have no intention to. Just hear me out though. You might read something of value that creates a drive to propel forward.

I've been a Christian ever since I can remember. My mother had my two siblings and me in church every Sunday and Bible study every Wednesday. As a kid, I never really understood the concept of religion and spirituality. But I remember praying by myself for the first time as a college student, preparing to take a college exam that would determine my eligibility to continue school. I was nervous, but my prayer gave me hope that everything would work out in my favor.

To make a long story short, I ended up passing the exam and was able to take my core classes. Connecting myself spiritually generates the peace, purpose, and forgiveness I needed to push through.

More tough times always seem to lie ahead, but connecting yourself spiritually equips you with the peace, purpose, and forgiveness you'll need to overcome those hardships. Religion and spirituality help you cope with difficult situations while also allowing you to identify life lessons and challenging situations. Although religion and spirituality work hand in hand, it is still possible to be spiritual without practicing religion. Spirituality just means that there is a sense of connection to something bigger than ourselves. It also enhances one's individuality by focusing on the connection to what they believe in and their own personal growth. However, I believe both practices play a major role in how you're able to deal with hardships. I suggest figuring out which practice works best for you and inserting it into your daily life.

DON'T BE AFRAID OF SITTING STILL

In chapter 5, I talked a little about meditation and practicing mindfulness, but I would like to go more in depth about meditation and learning to sit still. Have you ever heard the saying, "Just because you're busy doesn't mean you're productive"? As I've said before, I'm not big on cliché phrases because oftentimes they're not used correctly or are just overused. But this was something I could relate to and only learned from experience that always trying to keep myself busy usually was only moving me in circles. We often hear people mention the "grind" and instantly think by constantly moving we're moving forward, but in actuality we're just moving in circles.

That's why we get so frustrated when the outcome is not the outcome we expected. Being in grind mode for a while offers little to no results from all the work we put in—which has to be the worst feeling ever. Believe me, I know. I've been there plenty of times. Ask yourself, "When was the last time I stopped everything and just sat still?" When I mean sit still, I'm not talking about isolating yourself in your house all day. I'm talking about giving yourself a break from working on extracurricular projects and spending more time thinking and meditating on where you are in life and where you're trying to go.

This method of meditation is the most effective way to clear my mind of everything and focus on my next steps for moving forward with my career and making my next move my best move. The last eight or nine months of living in Columbus, Georgia, I decided to take a break from creative projects out of frustration and confusion when I found myself going in circles. It was best for me to sit still for a while and let my true purpose find me. Within those eight or nine months, I found clarity of purpose, and that's what prompted my move to Los Angeles. My mind was cleared of all distractions so that I was able to find clarity in the moment of being still.

By constantly moving and jumping from one thing to the next, we lose sight of where our true purpose lies. We begin to drift and involve ourselves in situations that take us away from our true purpose. When you find yourself lost in the midst of a "spin cycle," pull back. Put every project on hold and be okay with sitting still for a while. This brief period of stillness allows the mind to reset, and in the process, your true purpose is revealed.

GO ON AN ADVENTURE

My wife and I make it a priority every year to travel in the States or out of the country. It's one of our biggest stress relievers, but it also gives us a mental recharge to come back to the daily grind and be more motivated than ever to knock out our goals.

I get some of the best ideas being exposed to new places, people, and experiences while on vacation, expanding my mind while also broadening my perspective. Traveling forces you to think about your own culture and reevaluate your principles, values, and sometimes even have the new perspective change them.

While traveling to Costa Rica in 2018, I struck up a conversation with one of the employees at the resort and asked him if he'd ever traveled to the States. His answer was no because of the restrictions to get a passport as well as the cost. The next day, I struck up another conversation with two more employees and asked them the same question, and they both said the exact same thing. And I thought to myself, *Wow, I can't believe it's so hard for them to travel, whereas for Americans it's nothing to get a passport and travel all over the world.* As we were being transported to our excursions for the day, we drove through a lot of impoverished areas, and I was struck with a new appreciation for my country and my livelihood. This one-day experience changed my perspective on life. No matter what hardships I may have faced in my life, it was nothing compared to the economic hardships of these Costa Ricans. Keeping this in mind, I have been better able to deal with small obstacles and find solutions rather than problems.

Traveling affords me the opportunity to reflect on my life and where I'm headed next while also presenting new opportunities to reinvent myself. I mentioned before how I've come up with the best ideas while on vacation, but I'm also forced to meditate on the possibility of reinventing myself based on my experience and the skills I acquired throughout my journey. The Costa Rica trip came just a year after being laid off from the radio station. I knew there was a bigger purpose for me, and while on my trip to Costa Rica, I was able to think about all of the skills I've acquired over the years and how I could use those skills to do meaningful work.

I was forced to think about what I enjoyed doing, and that turned out to be creating content. I realized that the skills involved with creating content were the same skills I'd been using as both a producer and radio personality. I thought about my love for television and film and flirted with the idea of taking my talent to the film/TV world as a producer. I was a good writer, had mastered skills in interviewing, was familiar with using the editing software Final Cut, and had a knack for different television concepts. It was time to reinvent myself, and this was the trip I needed to reflect and open my mind to new opportunities. The vision was still fuzzy then, but it stayed with me until one day I found clarity in that vision. I haven't looked back since.

Just to be clear, going on an adventure does not have to be a trip out of the country. It could be a weekend getaway to another city where you enjoy new people, places, and adventures. The main point is that your surroundings are different, and you're temporarily escaping your old life, freeing your mind to reflect and opening your mind to alternative opportunities to stay in the race.

WEEK ELEVEN EXERCISES

This is a new week. Let's focus on renewing your mind by reflecting on your past experiences and taking a break from extracurricular activities for now.

Exercise One

Take this week and do some heavy thinking and reflecting on how far you've come to where you're at now. Refrain from working on your passion projects this week; instead, use the extra time to be mindful of your journey and look for where other opportunities can happen for you. If you can, try finding a peaceful place you can go to every day this week to put your ideas and experiences in perspective.

Exercise Two

Take yourself on an adventure for the weekend, whether it is just for the day or a three-day getaway. Find a new environment where you can experience new people and new activities. This could be a getaway to the other side of town, ziplining for the first time, or whatever you consider a new adventure that you always wanted to try. This exercise frees up your mind, allowing time for reflection and giving yourself perspective.

USE THE NEXT COUPLE OF PAGES TO COMPLETE THE EXERCISES

EXERCISE ONE

What was your life like five years ago? In what areas have you grown from then to now?

_____

_____

_____

_____

_____

_____

_____

_____

_____

_____

_____

_____

_____

EXERCISE TWO

Where did you go for your adventure? What new perspective did you gain?

_____

_____

_____

_____

_____

_____

_____

_____

_____

_____

_____

_____

_____

12

FINAL THOUGHTS

I t has taken me a year to flesh out all of my experiences and compile them, as well as my best practices to stay inspired, and carefully format them into a book. To be honest, at the time when I was living through the low points in my life, I had no clue that my responses to these hardships (the practices that I discussed in this book) were actually keeping me in the game. I just knew that failure wasn't an option, and my determination to win outweighed any obstacle in my way.

After I completed season one of *Become Inspired*, I began to meditate and reflect on the hardships I'd faced and what I did to stay inspired. As I continued to reflect, I realized these practices allowed me to withstand the mental breakdown of not being where I wanted to be. Instead, they allowed me to see a different perspective, which fueled my motivation to make it each day.

By implementing these practices into your life, you'll begin to notice a change in how you perceive certain hardships, and what would normally tear you down in defeat, you'll begin to look at it in a different light. I like to remind people when they vent to me about their struggles that the journey is more important than the destination. Where there is no struggle there is no growth. And when there is no growth, there is no progress.

One of the most important things for me to remember while on my journey is that things will never go as planned. But if I'm willing to adjust and pivot, I can find success right on the other side of disappointment. That goes for you as well. You can have the perfect plan for the next ten years of your life, but I can promise it will never go exactly as you've planned. You'll need to make adjustments or pivots to reach your end goal, and that's okay.

This book is a guide to staying inspired throughout your journey. I hope it gives you the support and constructive ideas you need to gain strong momentum as you take those necessary baby steps on the way to making your dreams a reality. Trust in the process and become inspired!

ABOUT THE AUTHOR

Jay Styles is an entrepreneur, author, and a TV/film producer—writing, producing, and directing entertainment that not only inspires but also brings awareness to the issues that are important and tells the stories that matter. Jay produced and directed his first docuseries, *Become Inspired*, in 2019, followed by a second season released May 8, 2020, on Amazon Prime Video. With fifteen years working in the entertainment industry, Jay has interviewed the likes of Denzel Washington, Forest Whitaker, Samuel L Jackson, Rosario Dawson, and Will Ferrell, to name a few. He got his early start as a radio personality in Columbus, Georgia, and later moved to Los Angeles where he spent six years as a producer for CBS radio and working as a weekend radio personality for 100.9 the Heat in Palmdale, California.

Jay, like many people, was forced to overcome countless financial and spiritual obstacles in his early years as a college student and throughout his professional career. If it weren't for prayer, the support of family and friends, and changing his mindset to take control of his destiny, he would not be able to truly live out his purpose. That purpose is to help you to push past your fears and awaken your inner greatness.

When Jay is not creating for television, he is traveling the world with his wife, searching for his next inspiration to motivate others on their journey toward greatness.

Follow Jay on social media
www.instagram.com/jaystylestv
www.facebook.com/jaystylestv
www.twitter.com/jaystylestv

NEED HELP TURNING YOUR TESTIMONY INTO A BOOK?

Join my Testimony to Life-Changing Book Course
"Learn How to Get Started in 9 Weeks and Change Lives

Contact me to learn more.

info@blackwallstreetpublishing.com

NOTES

_____

_____

_____

_____

_____

_____

_____

_____

_____

_____

_____

_____

_____

_____

_____

_____